Bees with Attitudes

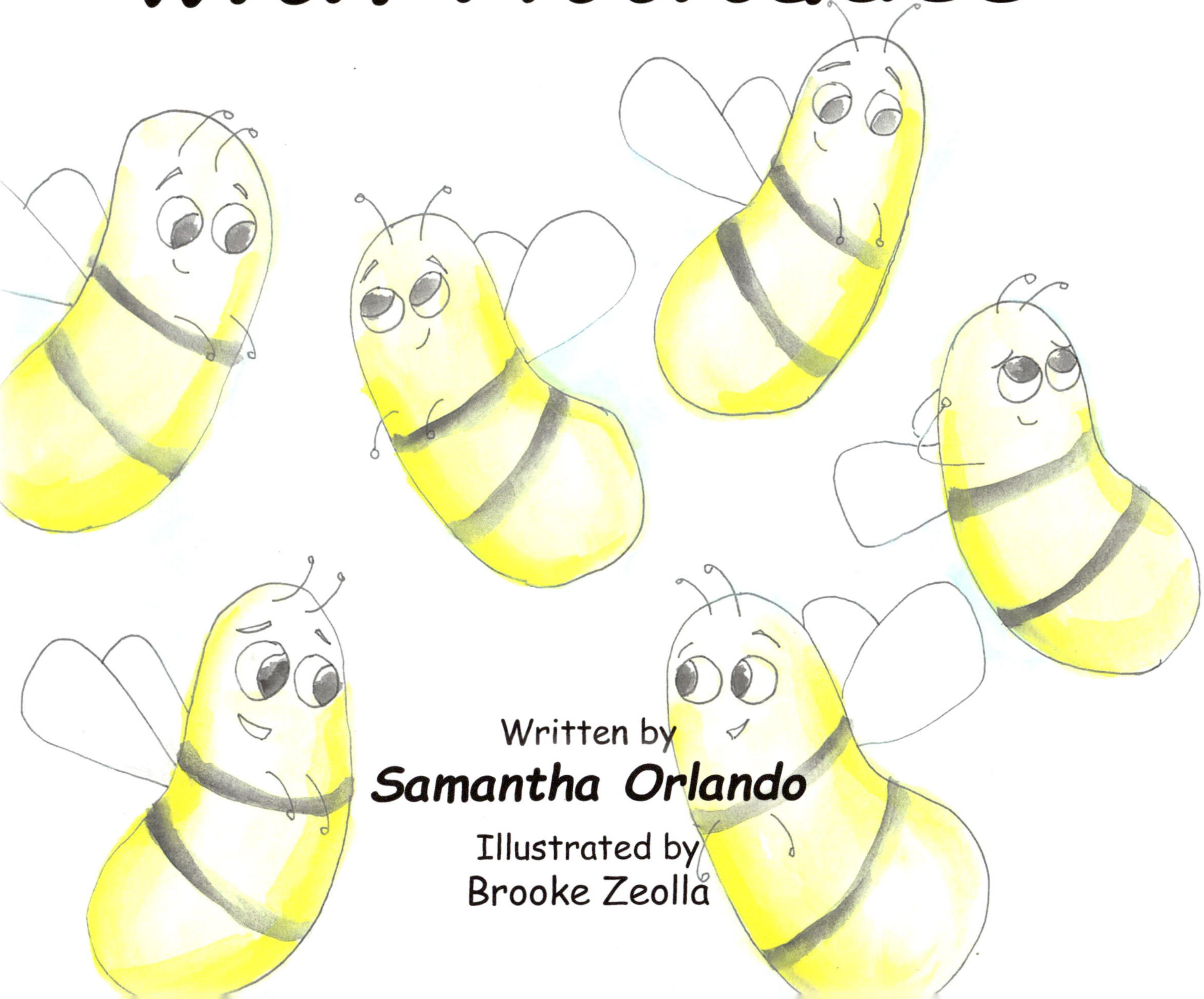

Written by
Samantha Orlando

Illustrated by
Brooke Zeolla

ISBN 979-8-88751-443-7 (paperback)
ISBN 979-8-88751-444-4 (digital)

Copyright © 2022 by Samantha Orlando

All rights reserved. No part of this publication may be reproduced, distributed, or transmitted in any form or by any means, including photocopying, recording, or other electronic or mechanical methods without the prior written permission of the publisher. For permission requests, solicit the publisher via the address below.

Christian Faith Publishing
832 Park Avenue
Meadville, PA 16335
www.christianfaithpublishing.com

Printed in the United States of America

About the Author and Illustrator

This book was a sister project. Samantha (24) and Brooke (21) are sisters who love the Lord and enjoy being creative. Samantha approached her sister Brooke about illustrating for a children's book the Lord had put on her heart. Samantha studied early childhood education, special education, and Christian counseling at Liberty University (class of 2019). Brooke studied interior design at the College for Creative Studies (class of 2022).

Samantha lives in Michigan. She married her husband Michael back in September of 2021, and they have three dogs: Ink the dachshund, Daisy the beagle, and Laila the pomsky. She graduated from Liberty University, class of 2019, with a bachelor's degree in early childhood education with a double minor in special education and Christian counseling. When she is not spending time with her family, she can be found gardening, painting, cooking or baking, or drinking coffee. She also enjoys being outside and going on adventures. Samantha's faith is extremely important to her, and she wants the Lord to be seen in all that she says and does. She loves the Lord, and her heart is to serve him.

Samantha also wanted to acknowledge her younger sister Brooke, who brought Samantha's drawings to life by illustrating for her book. Brooke graduated from the College for Creative Studies where she studied interior design (class of 2022). They have always been close, so it was a blessing for them to work together.

The inspiration for this book came from a memory that Samantha had about something she did as a child in Sunday school. All the children had little bumblebees with their pictures on them. Every Sunday, if they could tell their teacher about an opportunity they had during the week to show the Beatitudes to someone around them, they got to move their bees down the wall and get a prize. Samantha wants to encourage children to work at keeping these attitudes, along with a relationship with Jesus, so one day they can get the ultimate prize of heaven.

Bees with Attitudes is a story about a second-grade girl named Ruth and some bees who help her learn about the Beatitudes found in the Bible in the book of Matthew, chapter 5. The eight Beatitudes that Jesus teaches about in his Sermon on the Mount are the attitudes that Christians should have here on this Earth because they reflect Christ. The book begins with the Scripture reference of the Beatitudes.

In this story, Ruth and her second-grade class take a field trip to the most famous honey plant in her town to learn about the honey-making process. Ruth wanders off from the class and finds herself having conversations with some friendly bees. These bees begin to tell Ruth about why their honey is the best, and they tell her it is because of their attitudes. The bees then begin to tell Ruth about the Beatitudes in the Bible. Ruth is fascinated by what she learned and then tells her parents on her way home from the field trip. They help Ruth relate the bees and their attitudes to Jesus and our attitudes. At the end of the book, Ruth has a question for all the readers.

Message from the Author

Bees with Attitudes is a children's story about the Beatitudes found in the book of Matthew, chapter 5, on the attitude Christians are supposed to have here on this Earth. The inspiration came from something that I, Samantha, remember doing as a child in Sunday school. All the children had little bumblebees with our pictures on them. Every Sunday, if we could tell our teacher about an opportunity we had during the week to show the Beatitudes to someone around us, we got to move our bees down the wall and get a prize. I want to encourage children to work at keeping these attitudes, along with a relationship with Jesus, so one day they can get the ultimate prize of heaven.

Now when Jesus saw the crowds, he went up on a mountainside and sat down. His disciples came to him, and he began to teach them. He said: "Blessed are the poor in spirit, for theirs is the kingdom of heaven. Blessed are those who mourn, for they will be comforted. Blessed are the meek, for they will inherit the earth. Blessed are those who hunger and thirst for righteousness, for they will be filled. Blessed are the merciful, for they will be shown mercy. Blessed are the pure in heart, for they will see God. Blessed are the peacemakers, for they will be called children of God. Blessed are those who are persecuted because of righteousness, for theirs is the kingdom of heaven. "Blessed are you when people insult you, persecute you and falsely say all kinds of evil against you because of me. Rejoice and be glad, because great is your reward in heaven, for in the same way they persecuted the prophets who were before you.

—Matthew 5:1–12 NIV

It was a beautiful spring day when Ruth and her second-grade class were on their way to the most successful honey plant in their town. The entire class was excited about this trip, especially Ruth, who loves bees.

The town of Sunflower is famous for having the best honey in all the land. The plant's name is Heaven's Honey.

"We are here! We are here!" Ruth screamed with excitement as the bus pulled up to the plant.

The school bus doors opened, and Ruth ran straight for a tall man named Matthew, the beekeeper here at Heaven's Honey.

The rest of the children ran off the bus and toward the beekeeper, Matthew. Once their teacher, Miss Debbie, caught up to her class, Matthew introduced himself.

"Hello! My name is Matthew. Welcome to Heaven's Honey!

Let the tour begin!"

All the children followed him, except Ruth. She saw some bees near a tree and went to look at them.

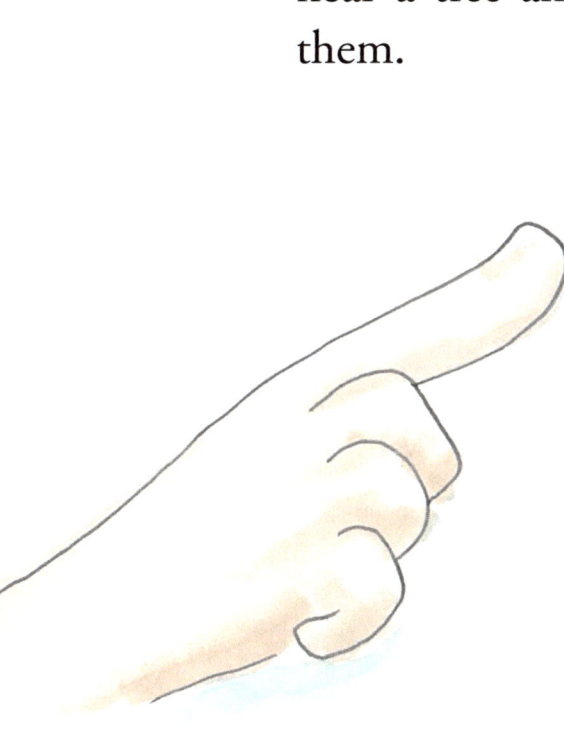

"Hello, pretty bees," Ruth said.

"My mom and dad say this place has the best honey in town, I wonder why?"

Ruth sat down under the tree and looked up at the giant hive.

Suddenly, eight bees flew down to meet Ruth.

"Hello, bees!" she said with a giant smile on her face. "I am Ruth, and I am seven."

"Hi, Ruth!" the bees said.

"We wanted to answer your question and tell you why Heaven's Honey is the best honey."

"Let me start," said the first bee. "I am poor in spirit."

Ruth looked confused.

The bee said, "It means humble."
"What does humble mean?" Ruth asked.

The bee said, "We are humble bees. Humble bees are not proud or stuck-up. Humble bees do not brag about how cool they are. Humble bees put other bees' needs before their own."

"Whoa! I want to be a humble bee," Ruth shouted.

"My turn! My turn!" the next bee said with excitement. "I am meek."

Ruth looked confused.

"Meek bees are patient bees," the bee said.

"Tell me more!" Ruth shouted.

I'M A PATIENT BEE!

The bee said, "Patient bees do not get mad or angry easily. Patient bees wait their turn without throwing a fit. Patient bees do not get annoyed all the time."

"Wow! I want to be a patient bee," Ruth said.

"My turn! My turn!" the next bee said.

"I am merciful. Merciful bees are loving and forgiving. Merciful bees are kind to other bees who are not kind to us."

"Ooh, I want to be a merciful bee!" Ruth said, yelling with excitement. "Wow! I did not know being a good bee meant all this."

"But wait, there is more, Ruth!" said one bee. "I am a peacemaker."

"I help other bees solve problems and avoid fights," said the bee.

"Cool!" Ruth said with excitement. "I will be a peacemaker for my brothers!"

"Me next!" another bee said. "I mourn."

Ruth looked confused. "Why?" she asked.

The bee said, "To mourn is like being sad. When I do something bad or something I know I should not do, I mourn because I know I messed up."

"So when I get in trouble, I should mourn?" Ruth asked.

The bee answered, "When we mourn for what got us in trouble, we are less likely to do that thing again."

Just as the next bee was about to speak to Ruth, Miss Debbie ran over.

"Ruth! There you are!" she said. "I have been looking all over for you. It is time to go."

"But I cannot go yet!" Ruth said. "I want to learn more from the bees!"

"I am sorry, Ruth, but it is time to go," Miss Debbie said.

Ruth got on the school bus with her class. She thought about what the bees told her, and she wanted to know more. She wondered if her parents knew what the bees were talking about and if they could help her.

When Ruth got back to school, her parents were there waiting to pick her up.

"Mom! Dad!" Ruth said. "I learned so much about Heaven's Honey and why it is the best today, but we had to leave before I could finish talking to the bees."

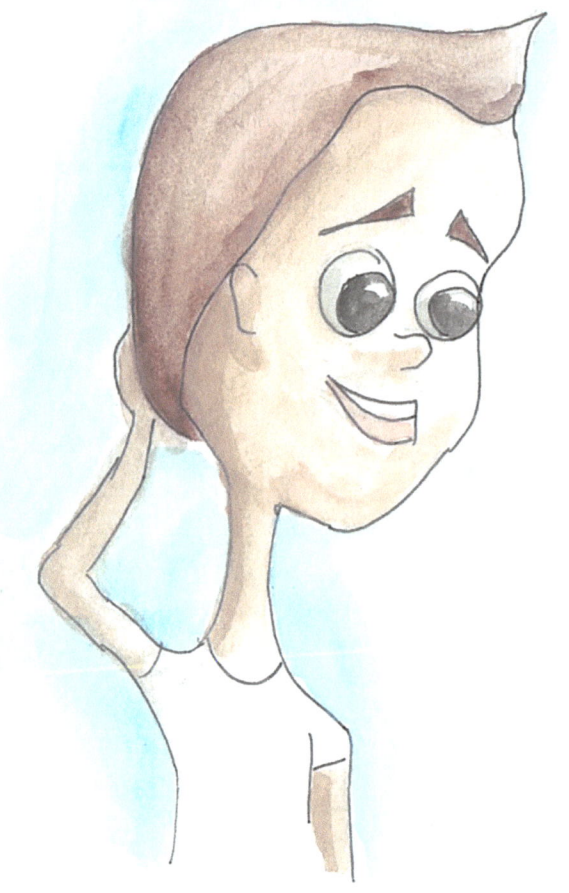

"You talked to bees?" her parents asked.

"Yes!" Ruth replied.

"They were teaching me about good attitudes! They said they were blessed bees because they were poor in spirit, and meek, and merciful, and that they mourn when they get in trouble, and that they are peacemakers."

Her parents looked at each other and smiled.

"Ruth," her parents said. "The bees were talking about the Beatitudes from the Bible."

"They were?" Ruth asked.

"Yes," her parents replied.
"And they left out the last three," they said.

"Do you know them?" Ruth asked excitedly.
"Yes!" her parents replied.
"The last three are about Jesus and wanting to be like him," they said.
"Jesus? The person we learn about at church?" Ruth asked.

Her parents said, "The last three Beatitudes are being pure in heart, hungering and thirsting for righteousness, and being persecuted for righteousness's sake."

"Those are really big words," Ruth said.

Her parents replied, "To be pure in heart is to think good thoughts and to keep our lives focused on Jesus. We should keep our lives and our minds clean of bad thoughts.

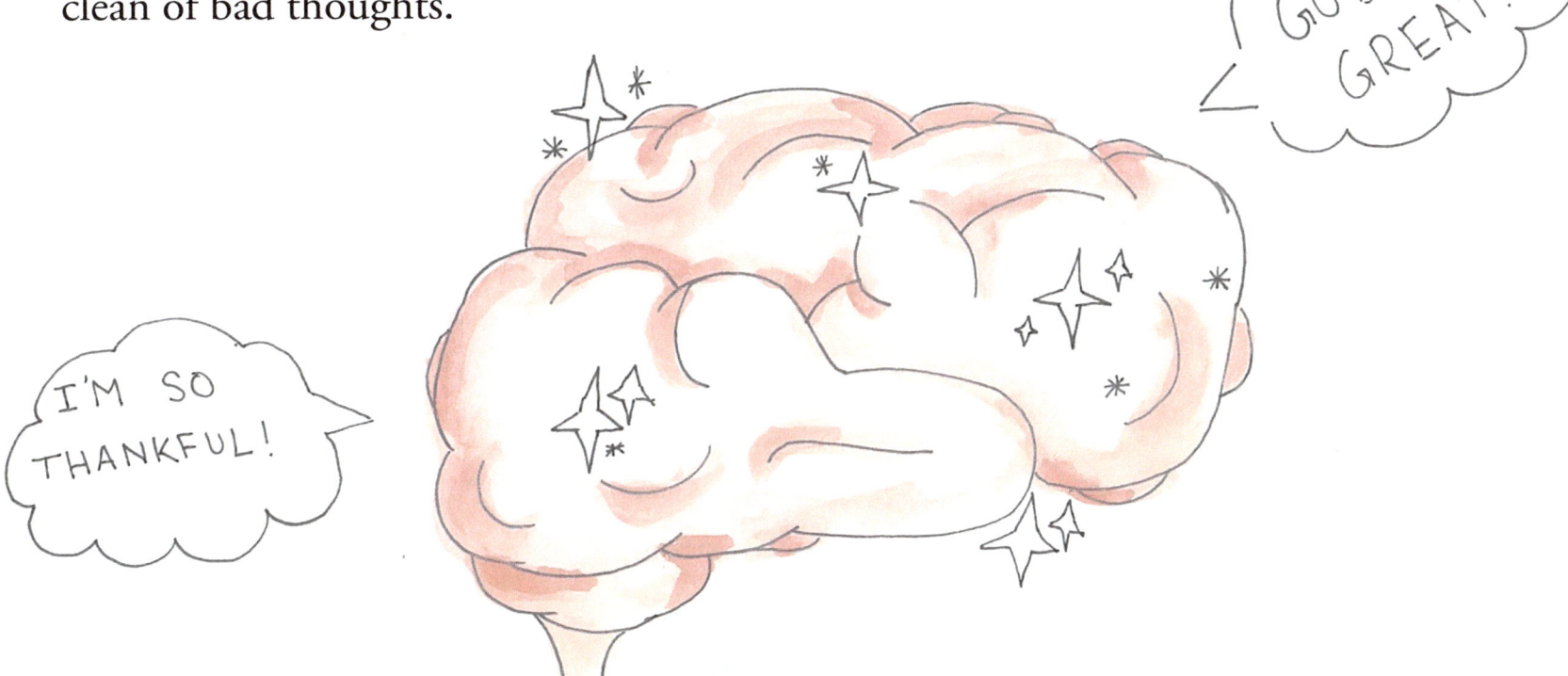

"To hunger and thirst for righteousness means to want to be like Jesus. Righteous is like perfect.

"And persecuted for righteousness' sake means that if someone makes fun of you or is mean to you because you love Jesus, it is okay. We should not be mad about it, but we should be happy," her parents said.

"Whoa!" Ruth replied. "So that is why Heaven's Honey is the best."

"Yes, exactly," her parents replied.

"The beekeeper, Matthew, goes to our church. He must have taught his bees to live out the Beatitudes to produce the best honey. Heaven's Honey is the best honey because Matthew taught his bees to follow Jesus's teachings."

Ruth replied, "So if I live with these same attitudes, what happens to me?"

Her parents said, "If you live out the Beatitudes, your reward will be in heaven, and the attitude you have here on Earth will point others to Jesus."

Ruth smiled.

"If you think Heaven's Honey tastes good, wait until you have the honey up in heaven. It will be even sweeter," her parents said.

So now that Ruth knows what attitudes she should have in this world, she tries her best every day to be humble, patient, forgiving, loving, peaceful, and mournful of bad things, and she tries to be like Jesus no matter what anyone else says.

Ruth wants to know if you will join her.

Will you be like the bees who have good attitudes?

Printed in the USA
CPSIA information can be obtained
at www.ICGtesting.com
LVHW061532081024
793248LV00004B/69